Hmong Learning *series*

BABY *numbers*

let's learn Hmong together!

let's learn Hmong together!

mai nhia yang

Vang Publishing House

Cover Design: Mai Nhia Yang

First Edition
Published by Vang Publishing House

ISBN: 978-1-972879-12-2

Printed in United States of America

www.vangpublishinghouse.com

Dedication

This book is lovingly dedicated to the children and families who carry the beauty of the Hmong language and culture forward each day.

May these pages bring joy, connection, and pride as you learn, grow, and count together.

To every child discovering their voice, and to every parent, caregiver, and educator guiding them. This book is for you.

A Guide for Parents & Caregivers

Thank you for choosing this book to support your child's early learning journey.

Learning numbers is one of the first steps in building strong foundational skills in early childhood. In this book, children are introduced to numbers in both English and Hmong, helping to support language development while also strengthening cultural identity.

You can use this book in simple and meaningful ways:

• Read together
Point to each number and say it out loud in both languages.
Encourage your child to repeat after you.

• Count with objects
Use everyday items like toys, snacks, or steps to practice counting in real life.

• Take your time
Children learn best through repetition. It's okay to revisit the same page again and again.

• Make it interactive
Ask questions like, "Can you find three things?" or "Let's count together!"

• Celebrate effort
Learning a new language or strengthening one takes time. Celebrate every attempt and progress your child makes.

This book was created to be simple, engaging, and meaningful, so that learning feels natural and joyful.

1

One

Ib

2

Two

Ob

3

Three

Peb

4

Four

Plaub

IXAT

5

Five

Tsib

6

Six

Rau

7

Seven

Xya

8

Eight

Yim

9

Nine

Cuaj

10

Ten

Kaum

11

Eleven

Kaum Ib

12

Twelve

Kaum Ob

13

Thirteen

Kaum Peb

14

Fourteen

Kaum Plaub

Beans

Soup

Peas

Tomatoes

Tuna

Corn

Chicken

Pineapple

Fruit

Pasta Sauce

Carrots

Olives

Mushrooms

Pumpkin

15

Fifteen

Kaum Tsib

16

Sixteen

Kaum Rau

17

Seventeen

Kaum Xya

A
B
C
4

18

Eighteen

Kaum Yim

19

Nineteen

Kaum Cuaj

20

Twenty

Nees Nkaum

About the Author & Illustrator

Mai Nhia Yang is an early childhood educator with a deep passion for helping young children learn through culture, language, and play. Through her work, she strives to create meaningful learning experiences that support early development while honoring identity and heritage.

As both the author and illustrator of this book, Mai Nhia brings together education and creativity to make learning Hmong numbers engaging, simple, and joyful for children and families.

www.ingramcontent.com/pod-product-compliance
Lightning Source LLC
LaVergne TN
LVHW070150110826
845147LV00002B/368

9781972879122